INVITATION TO TEA GARDENS

Kyoto's Culture Enclosed

Preston L. Houser/Mizuno Katsuhiko

MITSUMURA SUIKO SHOIN

■ CONTENTS

35	*Ninna-ji*	¥350	9:00〜4:30	Ukyo-ku Omuro Ouchi 33
36	*Ryoan-ji*	¥350	8:00〜5:00	Ukyo-ku Ryoan-ji Goryo Shitamachi 13
37,38	*Saiho-ji*	By appointment		Nishikyo-ku Matsuo Jingatani-cho
39	*Murin-an*	¥200	9:00〜4:30	Sakyo-ku Nanzen-ji Kusagawa-cho
40	*Saiko-ji*	By appointment		Kita-ku Murasakino Rendaino-cho 15
41	*Ryosoku-in*	By appointment		Higashiyama-ku Yamatooji dori Shijo-sagaru
42〜44	*Kodai-ji*	¥500	9:00〜4:00	Higashiyama-ku Shimo Kawaramachi Dori Yasaka Torii Mae Sagaru
45	*Kainyo-an*	By appointment		Higashiyama-ku Maruyama-koen Ongakudo Minamigawa
46	*Fushimi-Inari Shrine*	No charge for garden viewing		Fushimi-ku Fukakusa Yabunouchi-cho 68
47	*Higashi Hongan-ji*	By appointment		Shimogyo-ku Karasuma dori Shichijo-agaru

INVITATION TO TEA GARDENS

Kyoto's Culture Enclosed

Sixth Printing May 2002 by Mitsumura Suiko Shoin Co., Ltd.
Kitayama-dori Horikawa higashi-iru Kita-ku, Kyoto 603-8115 Japan
PHONE 075-493-8244
FAX   075-493-6011

Photographs: ©1992 Mizuno Katsuhiko
Text: ©1992 Preston L. Houser
Editor: Yasuhiro Asano
Design: Akira Shibagaki
Publisher: Kozo Nagasawa

ISBN4-8381-0116-3

THE TEA GARDEN

Kyoto's Culture Enclosed

京都茶の庭

写真　水野克比古

Photographs by Mizuno Katsuhiko

1 Omote Senke
表千家中潜

2 Omote Senke
表千家残月亭前露地

3　Omote Senke
表千家不審菴露地

4 Omote Senke
表千家祖堂前露地

5   Ura Senke
裏千家兜門より玄関への
霰零し露地

6 Ura Senke
裏千家寒雲亭前露地

7　Ura Senke
裏千家又隠前露地

8 Ura Senke
裏千家又隠東庭

9   Mushanokoji Senke
武者小路千家官休庵露地

10 Mushanokoji Senke
　　武者小路千家編笠門

11　Mushanokoji Senke
武者小路千家祖堂露地

12 Yabunouchi Shoke
藪内宗家燕庵前蹲踞

13 Katsura Rikyu
桂離宮松琴亭腰掛待合と延段

14 Katsura Rikyu

桂離宮松琴亭北、洲浜・天の橋立

15 Katsura Rikyu
桂離宮松琴亭東、石橋・流れ手水

16 Katsura Rikyu
桂離宮松琴亭北、土庇内

17　Sento Gosho
仙洞御所又新亭中門

18 Sento Gosho
仙洞御所又新亭露地

19　Sento Gosho
仙洞御所醒花亭北庭

20 Sento Gosho
仙洞御所醒花亭東庭

21   Koto-in
高桐院露地

22 Koto-in
高桐院松向軒内部

23　Koho-an
孤篷庵忘筌露地

24 Koho-an
孤篷庵山雲床蹲踞

25　Shinju-an
真珠庵庭玉軒露地

26 Shinju-an
真珠庵庭玉軒内部

27 Korin-in
興臨院涵虚亭露地

28　Saio-in
西翁院澱看の席露地

29　Koetsu-ji
光悦寺太虚庵光悦垣

30 Jikko-in
実光院理覚庵待合

31 Hokyo-ji
宝鏡寺三白社露地

32 Honen-in
法然院如意庵露地

33 Keishun-in
桂春院既白軒露地

34 Toji-in
等持院庭園と清漣亭

35 Ninna-ji
仁和寺遼廓亭蹲踞

36　Ryoan-ji
龍安寺蔵六庵蹲踞

37 Saiho-ji
西芳寺湘南亭露地

38 Saiho-ji
西芳寺湘南亭露地

39　Murin-an
無鄰菴庭園と茶室無鄰菴

40 Saiko-ji
西向寺松蔭席露地

41　Ryosoku-in
　両足院庭園と
　水月亭・臨池亭

42　Kodai-ji
高台寺遺芳庵露地

43　Kodai-ji
高台寺遺芳庵蹲踞

44 Kodai-ji
高台寺傘亭内部

45　Kainyo-an
皆如庵露地

46 Fushimi-Inari Shrine
伏見稲荷大社松の下屋庭園と瑞芳軒

47　Higashi Hongan-ji
東本願寺渉成園蹲踞

INVITATION TO TEA GARDENS

Kyoto's Culture Enclosed

by

Preston L. Houser

Dedication

To my wife, Michiyo,
who first introduced me to the world of tea.

I The Spirit of Tea

This past summer, my wife and I (with our young son in back pack) climbed Mt. Tallac, a modest 10,000 ft. peak just south west of Lake Tahoe in the California Sierra Nevada. From the trailhead, our view of the summit—with the anticipation of the day's trek—was a humble experience. Standing at the foot of the mountain we felt that it is true: mountains <u>are</u> enlightened Buddhas. The feeling was not unlike what is experienced when one enters the tea garden, or *roji,* for the first time, or the thousandth time. As we reflected momentarily on the expanse of our spirit—in the presence of an equal expanse of granite—we agreed that this was the spirit one should bring to the tea room.

The spirit is an empty one: ready again to be impressed with the values of an aesthetic and spiritual tradition that transcends, as well as enlightens, our modern age. A walk through a tea garden is a walk through time as much as it is through space: it prepares the spirit to receive again, through a cup of tea, an aesthetic experience of profound dimensions. And yet, how is this done? The garden does not attempt to represent nature in its natural state, the tea house is not the epitome of architectural development, and the tea ceremony itself does not test the limits of physical dexterity or endurance. Still, we return from our tea enriched. The world of tea serves as a reflection of human, i.e. symbolic, culture at its most profound. This "Epiphany," as it were, is accomplished with asymmetry, antiquity, and a non-representation of the material gains which have tattooed the twentieth century.

Japanese history, art, and cultural complexity, can be condensed into a single gesture: the tea ceremony. On the surface, this condensation might symbolize Japan's current international reputation for making things small, and yet what is projected is not a mere miniaturization of action and spirit, but rather a concentration of heritage and aesthetic values into an intricate symphony of movement which, in concert with the guests, the environment, and the tea itself, produces an apotheosis of spiritual and artistic expression.

The Tea Ceremony, *Cha-no-yu,* or *Sado,* as it is known in Japan, is still practiced by a large percentage of the population: mostly women. It is still socially recognized as an important requisite for married life—again, at least for women (*hanayome-shugyo*). A bride adept at serving tea promises to provide the proper environment necessary for today's modern, over-worked, and frantic family. The advantages of knowing such a skill are as concrete as they are spiritual: when the senses are relaxed, alert, and receptive, the demons of chaos and destruction are less threatening. What better way to unite and strengthen a family, or community, than by sharing a cup of tea?

There are four spiritual and artistic components essential to the world of tea: "harmony" ("*wa*"), "reverence" ("*kei*"), "purity" ("*sei*"), and "tranquility" ("*jaku*"). Throughout the tea garden, tea room, and the ceremony itself are symbolic representations of these elements: water drawn from the stone basin, *chozubachi,* is considered particularly pure; the act of crouching before the washing area, *tsukubai,* is an act of reverence; the garden should project a sense of harmony rarely found in daily life; awareness for the spirit of tea in turn produces a tranquility unknown to most artistic and spiritual endeavors. The qualities of harmony, reverence, purity, and tranquility are intimately entwined throughout all aspects of the tea world.

Although the above terms may be unknown to those outside the tea world, there are two notoriously enigmatic words which often grace intellectual discourse on the art of tea, and deserve further consideration: *wabi* and *sabi*. The word *wabi* comes from the adjective *wabishi*, which translates as "solitude" or one preferring solitude over companionship. When considering art, an object said to possess the characteristics of *wabi* would be asymmetrical, rustic, and imperfect, or, in other words, alienated from the norm. What is suggested is not innocence or naivete, but rather a primitive quality which reflects a deeper spiritual context. Imperfection as an aesthetic quality implies that the eye of the beholder, as it were, brings the object to perfection. Material perfection, by contrast, signals the end of the beholder's involvement with the art form. *Wabi* destroys the framework which would otherwise promote a sense of systematic perfection.

In metaphysical terms, *wabi* denotes a kind of spiritual poverty, but must not be associated with depravity. Rather, what is implied is a non-dependency on worldly things. It is a state a grace to which many of us aspire. (However, we usually feel it will be achieved as soon as we acquire one more, final possession, which, of course, isolates us even further from our goal.) Perhaps a more accurate definition would be spiritual austerity: a conscientious condition which affords no waste of thought or movement. For Americans, Henry David Thoreau, and his experiences which produced Walden, might be said to embody the characteristics of *wabi*. Closer to our own era, the spirit of *wabi* may be defined in the words of American poet and former Kyoto resident, Gary Snyder: "True affluence is not needing anything."

Sabi, on the other hand, evokes an image of solitude or loneliness, but again not to suggest deprivation. *Sabi* comes from an adjective describing loneliness (*sabishi*). Yet, *sabi* also reflects a sense of antiquity or primitiveness that an object, for instance, pottery or other tea utensils, may possess. An object which exists self-contained, outside the sphere of an arbitrarily decided standard of aesthetic excellence, could be said to possess *sabi*. Indeed, an object thought to embody the qualities of *sabi* would inspire the beholder to abandon feelings of desire for that object. As James Joyce wrote in Portrait of the Artist as a Young Man, true art is static in that, in its presence, the mind is arrested and raised above desire and loathing. The rest, he wrote, is pornography.

Wabi and *sabi* are often used interchangeably, but there is an important difference: *wabi* is the result of a decisive, willful action, or, as mentioned above, a preference; whereas *sabi* describes a found condition. Together, *wabi* and *sabi* represent the spiritual condition necessary to fully appreciate the subtleties of tea. The spiritual condition, (as suggested by Joyce, Snyder, and the tea and Zen masters who follow) is an emptiness—*sunyata* in Sanskrit—which allows the many forms of God, truth, or enlightenment to be realized.

II Tea Masters

The history of the tea ceremony is irrevocably linked with the tea masters which developed it. Any study of tea must begin from a standpoint of practically a "cult of personality" surrounding those who first propagated the art form.

The tea ceremony, as we know it today, is primarily a result of the aesthetic insights of Sen-no-Rikyu (1521-1591). Rikyu taught that the art of *chanoyu* consists in nothing else but in boiling water, making tea and sipping it. There were others prior to Sen-no-Rikyu, however: Japanese Zen pioneer Eisai (1141-1215); national teacher Muso Kokushi (1275-1351); the illustrious poet, calligrapher, and abbot of Daitoku-ji Ikkyu Sojun (1394-1481); Ikkyu's student Murata Shuko (1422-1502); and Rikyu's master Takeno Joo (1502-1555) were the most influential tea masters in the history of tea.

Eisai is first credited with encouraging the consumption of tea among his compatriots to prolong life and promote a healthy constitution. He noted how Japan is "full of sickly-looking, skinny persons, and this is simply because we do not drink tea." Although he did not teach the way to perform the tea ceremony, he did much to popularize the art of drinking tea among the Zen and warrior, *samurai*, elite of the day. But it was Ikkyu (who, among other things, preferred brothels to traditional training halls for Zen meditation*) who first suggested to his disciple, Shuko, that tea and Zen Buddhism be combined. Murata Shuko—sometimes referred to as Juko—is said to have raised the tea ceremony to an art form, and is responsible for preparing the tea world for Sen-no-Rikyu. Shuko isolated tea from the more mundane environment of private residences or temple rooms and placed the tea room in its own environment, the *sukiya*, or tea house. He is also credited with introducing the four and a half tatami mat room (*yo-jo-han*) as a standard size for the practice of tea. He even tried to integrate bathing into the tea ceremony! Perhaps his most profound contribution to the art of tea was his cultivation of the aesthetic of *wabi*: that elusive quality of tea through which so much is understood. It was Shuko who, as Sonja Arntzen writes, "originated the 'grass hut' style of tea ceremony, the style that was passed on to Sen no Rikyu and thence handed down as the classical form of tea." With the "grass hut" style, tea began to separate itself from ordinary social endeavors, and develop as a spiritual pursuit.

Takeno Joo followed Shuko, and like Muso Kokushi, was involved in local politics as well as becoming a renown tea teacher (a combination of priorities which were to prove fatal to Rikyu). Joo came from a wealthy family of Sakai tanners. At the time, Sakai was one of Japan's busiest ports of what is now Osaka, and it served as the gateway through which the arts of China entered Japan. The art of tea, which came from Ming China, made its way through Sakai during the Muromachi era (1334-1568), hence making the merchant class of the region not only culturally sophisticated, but also wealthy. (To this day, the people of Osaka have inherited an inflated reputation for business acumen.) As the art of tea gained popularity, the affluent merchants of Sakai became infamous for the extravagant sums paid for tea paraphernalia.

This brings us to Sen-no-Rikyu. Like his teacher, Rikyu was born to a wealthy merchant family of Sakai. Having completed his studies under Takeno Joo's tutelage, Rikyu, at age 50, was given his Buddhist tea name by Emperor Ogimachi, in recognition of his mastery of the art of tea. Rikyu infused such a sense of spirituality into the art of tea that it was elevated from a simple past-time to "a Way of truth," and it is for this reason that he is revered among tea practitioners everywhere. A flamboyant personality, anecdotes about Rikyu abound: once after Rikyu's master, presumably Joo, had diligently swept the *roji* of dust and debris, he asked Rikyu to do the same. Upon finding a spotless garden and seeing his master's face, Rikyu knew just what to do; shaking a small tree, a few leaves fell to the ground; this pleased the master. Another time, Rikyu chastised his own son because one stepping stone in the garden was slightly higher than the rest. His son quickly and discreetly repaired the incongruity.

Rikyu eventually became politically linked with Oda Nobunaga and Toyotomi Hideyoshi, two of Japan's most dynamic leaders of the day. At a time in Japanese history when the conquest of the capital, Kyoto, owed as much to aesthetic mastery as to military might, arts of such grace as tea became powerful weapons and were intensely coveted. Hideyoshi, like Nobunaga before him, was an ardent admirer of Rikyu's, and he often used the tea ceremony as a pretense for clandestine political meetings. Undoubtedly, Rikyu was privy to many otherwise secret discussions. After rising in stature among the power elite in Kyoto, Rikyu was forced to commit *seppuku* (ritual suicide: an honor usually reserved for disgraced *samurai*) by Hideyoshi. The reasons remain vague to this day. It is thought that Hideyoshi had taken a fancy to Rikyu's widowed daughter. While still in mourning and having several children to look after, she did not respond favorably to Hideyoshi's advances. When Rikyu himself was ordered to deliver his daughter to Hideyoshi, his response was also not favorable, and considerably more blunt. This episode probably contributed to Rikyu and Hideyoshi's decaying friendship—which was also not helped by the latter's fear for his line of succession which prompted, among other acts of paranoic cruelty in his later life, an order to exterminate his adopted son Hidetsugu and his family. One day, while Hideyoshi was entering Daitoku-ji, he noticed on the second floor of the Sanmon Gate a statue of Rikyu. Outraged at having Rikyu look down on him, Hideyoshi ordered Rikyu confined to his house in Sakai. One month later Rikyu received the order to commit *seppuku*, which he calmly did after composing two death poems—one in Chinese and one in Japanese—and having a last cup of tea. The poems, from the Chinese and Japanese respectively, are loosely translated by D.T. Suzuki as follows:

Seventy years of life—
Ha ha! and what a fuss!
With this sacred sword of mine,
Both Buddhas and Patriarchs I kill!

III The Garden

I raise the sword,
This sword of mine,
Long in my possession—
The time is come at last—
Skyward I throw it up!

This was in 1591; Rikyu was 71 years old; Shakespeare was just beginning his career as a playwright.

After Rikyu, the most influential tea master was his disciple Furuta Oribe (1544-1615). Oribe's ideas on tea and especially the garden were to have lasting effects. Oribe felt that Rikyu's garden was maintained in an overly rustic fashion, and he tried to place trees and stones in more pleasing, albeit contrived, positions. (Rikyu had one tea garden which contained no stones whatsoever, merely grass growing every which way!) It is thought that from Oribe the idea of dividing the garden into sections with fences (*ai-no-gaki*) and small gates gained acceptance. Oribe also first suggested that stone lanterns (*toro*) be carved with figures of the Buddha. And, Oribe systemized much of the design of garden stones (*tobi ishi and shiki ishi*).

* *In all fairness it should be stressed that Ikkyu, like Milton, confronted head-on the challenges that sexuality places upon religious institutions and adepts; he saw sexuality (like Milton saw temptation) as an opportunity to investigate the dichotomy between spiritual and secular desires.*

Before we take up the more spiritual aspect of the garden and Zen, one point needs to be stressed, even at the risk of over-stating the obvious: the garden is a representation of Nature only insofar as natural artifacts are concerned. Symbolically, the garden is meant to incorporate natural and manmade materials to mirror and contribute to our understanding of human consciousness, (which, ironically, is rarely assumed to be willfully "manmade"). Rocks, plants and water, are used as simple materials for the artist to express strictly human values. There is no attempt to represent Nature *per se*. In fact, the garden represents everything wilderness is not. Like the arts of *bonsai*, or *ikebana*, nature is controlled, manipulated and compartmentalized to purely human ideals of nature. In this century, we have gained a deeper understanding, and—one hopes—respect for our planet's wild areas; yet the tea world's understanding and use of Nature by no means invalidates the spiritual experience to be had when visiting a tea garden.

That said, what then does the garden mean to us? How does one now approach the garden, knowing that what is found there is environmentally "unrealistic?" The conspicuous absence of Nature in its own terms means that we now approach the garden in human, i.e. symbolic, terms. The garden now begins to mean more than rock, plant, water, and air: we have entered the world of metaphor. In the garden, as in the tea room, nothing is left to chance: all is deliberately positioned. Like a carefully sculpted configuration, no allowance is made for the whims of the gods or wild nature. The garden serves the human soul. It is a secular stage where upon our spirituality is brought into play and reflected back to us.

It was not always this way. Shinto, the indigenous and animistic religion of Japan, is usually credited with providing the framework for the development of Taoist and Buddhist thought, and by extension, aesthetic development. Two main articles form the basis of Shinto thought: purity, and divine inhabitation of inanimate objects. For example, Shinto rites of purity are conducted in designated areas which are unmolested by human contact; mountains, stones, water, trees, etc., are home to countless gods and goddesses. It is thought that the landscape gardens which gradually formed an integral part of shrines, temples, and private residences, may have begun as an appreciation of the sacred sites of Shinto. Certainly, in Japan, the notion that the garden may represent something more sublime than simply rocks and bushes originates with Shinto. Yet, the garden became less an extension of sacred Nature, and more like an oasis in the city: islands of green amid the congestion of a developing society. People went to the shrine garden for "the view" rather than for a sense of participation with Nature. This disassociation from Nature continues today: in a Shinto shrine, within the tiny tract of untouchable land reserved for a god or a tomb of a departed emperor, we often find ourselves staring like spectators, at an ancient ecology, now caged as if in a zoo.

In any event, from its Shinto beginnings, the garden developed into the landscape art form we recognize today. David Slawson, in his book *Secret Teachings in the Art of Japanese Gardens* points to three aesthetic elements which influence the design of the Japanese garden: the scenic, the sensual, and the cultural. The scenic garden strives to recreate a scene of historical or nostalgic import. In an almost snap-shot fashion, whole mountain ranges are symbolically reduced to a handful of precisely placed stones; oceans and rivers are alluded to by carefully constructed ponds and streams. For example, the detached garden at Katsura boasts a recreated *Amanohashidate*, or "Bridge of Heaven." [see plates # 14 and 15] (One of the three most famous views of Japan along with Matsushima to the north and Miyajima to the south, *Amanohashidate* is a natural, pine-tree clad, sand-bar located on the Tango peninsula north-west of Kyoto.)

From a more sensual standpoint, however, most landscape gardens are designed with one of two distinct points of reference: "the view garden" and "the stroll garden." The view garden was originally conceived as a three dimensional painting to compliment a large room of a temple or residence. From the room one looked out upon the garden from a fixed point of reference, and the garden was arranged accordingly to provide maximum enjoyment for the viewers. While the garden was not strictly off-limits to strolling or boating, its main function was one of strict (and stationary) visual enjoyment. With the advent of the tea ceremony and the tea garden in the sixteenth and seventeenth centuries, there soon developed what came to be known as "the stroll garden" (*chisenkaiyu*). Instead of a single vantage point, as one strolled through the garden, a series of ever changing perspectives and vistas are presented to the viewer.

From these beginnings the tea garden, or *roji* as we

know it today, began. In a way, the *roji* rejects the systematic design of more conventional gardens. True, the design of the tea garden strives for an effect: that of focusing the guest's attention on the more sublime qualities of the tea ceremony, instead of a strictly pleasing visual experience. Around 1600, this idea of garden aesthetics was simply revolutionary. Tea masters realized the esoteric ideals that the tea ceremony sought to convey could be accomplished with less, rather than more, attention to the mechanics of traditional garden design.

The garden is more than our introduction to the tea world: it is an introduction to our original spirit. The *roji* ("dewy path") is the walkway by which we reach the tea room from the waiting area, figuratively as well as literally. The *roji*—which traces its etymology back to the Sanskrit—spiritually prepares the guest for the experience of the tea room. It signifies, as Kakuzo Okakura pointed out in his landmark treatise *The Book of Tea*, "the first stage of meditation—the passage into self-illumination." Okakura continues by explaining that the *roji* was intended to break connection with the outside world. More than an escape the tea garden offers a spiritual perspective which would be otherwise unavailable in the everyday world. Shoshitsu Sen XV elaborates by referring to a parable from the Lotus Sutra wherein a "father calls his children from a burning house to safety in the *roji*." Metaphorically, the burning house represents the suffering world, and the *roji* a sanctuary. In light of recent events at Three Mile Island, Chernobyl, and Mihama, we realize that our house is literally on fire! The *roji*, therefore, maintains a symbolic, historical, and contemporary introduction to the spiritual dimensions of the the tea ceremony.

The tea garden, or *roji*, is oriented to the guest's experience, not exclusively to the senses. While the tea garden is undoubtedly beautiful, the elements which go into creating a tea garden are directed toward making the guest's journey, from the waiting area to the tea room, as unobtrusive as possible. As one enters the garden, one is led to the waiting area, *machiai*. Here, the guest sits on a bench, *koshikake*, until called for. If necessary, the lavatory, *setchin*, is nearby. The *roji* is usually divided into two parts: the outer garden, *soto roji*, and the inner garden, *uchi roji*. (Generally, the *soto roji* is of rocky or sandy design, while the *uchi roji* is more verdant.) When one is called for the tea ceremony, one proceeds toward the middle gate, *naka kuguri*. If this is a formal tea ceremony, the host, *teishu*, will greet the guest at this point. This greeting is called *mukae-tsuke*, and it serves an important function in establishing the role of host and guest, as well as clarifying the spirits of giving and receiving. There are several types of middle gate: the thatched roof style, *kayabuki*, and the cypress bark style, *hiwadabuki*. In any case, one must stoop slightly to pass under the gate. This encourages the humble attitude necessary for one's progress toward the tea room.

Once inside the inner garden, the path to the tea room is rarely straight. The stepping stones are conscientiously set at a certain height and distance from each other: not only to provide the visual enjoyment of the seeing the pattern of stones on the ground, but also to deliberately influence the pace at which one walks toward the tea house, *sukiya*. The placement of the stepping stones, for example, is of crucial importance: height and distance between stones were meticulously considered, as the story of Rikyu and his son illustrates. Even today the height of the stones varies from school to school. There are two basic arrangements of the stepping stones: the cobblestone, or flagstone style, *shiki ishi*; and the more loosely arranged stepping stones, *tobi ishi*. The stones should be easy to walk on, but not in a straight line: that would be uninteresting. Nor should the stones draw attention to themselves, either by color or obvious expense. A.L. Sadler in *Cha-no-yu: The Japanese Tea Ceremony*, points out that there are even three types of stones to avoid: "diseased stones," those distorted at the top; "dead stones," horizontal stones that look like vertical ones which have fallen over; and "pauper stones," those which stand off by themselves with no relation to the others. Stones occupy different stages of importance throughout the garden. For example, the *kyaku ishi* is used for guests to rest their feet while waiting, and the *maeishi*, at the foot of the water basin.

It is in the inner garden, *uchi roji*, that one purifies oneself at the washing area, *tsukubai*. Coming to the *tsukubai*, the guest pauses at the large stone, *maeishi*, before the stone water basin, *chozubachi*. The area of purification is set deliberately at a low level so that one must crouch down to perform one's ablutions. (The origin of the word *tsukubai* comes from the verb "to crouch." See glossary.) The approach to the *tsukubai* was thoroughly considered so as to make one's cleansing of hands and mouth as poignant an experi-ence as possible. Since cleanliness and purity are spiritual virtues necessary to our experience of tea, water is used to represent these virtues. Always, summer and winter, a bucket of fresh water is kept to the side of the *chozubachi*. Water is present in the tea garden, but it must not assume the elaborate associations of scene that inform other landscape gardens, such as flowing streams. (Rikyu felt that the first order of business for the tea host is "water carrying." Initially, of course, water is carried to the *chozubachi*. But then, before the guests arrive, water, *uchi-mizu*, is sprinkled about the garden: first, thirty minutes before the guests arrive, then again, fifteen minutes before arrival, to insure that the water has evaporat-ed to the proper proportion.) A ladle made of bam-boo, *tsukubai bishaku*, is provided for the guests. After hands and mouth have been rinsed, one may proceed to the tea room, *chashitsu*, which is often only a few feet away. The walk through the garden should resemble a leisurely, but conscientious, stroll along a mountain path: after all, one has just entered the enlightened world, Nirvana. The relaxed feeling of the guest should concentrated, but not preoccupied, or distracted by ornate displays of flowers, trees, stones, or running water. (How many flowers can you find in the photographs?)

As the guest approaches the tea room, what has been experienced through the garden path has been nothing short of a dance re-enacting the calm and focused attention of the soul. We are now ready to partake in a cup of tea.

As suggested, since it is the way through the garden which is given priority, the *roji* has become a powerfully symbolic environment for tea guests and practitioners alike. It has become a sacred ground for a rite of passage of the most profound psychological implications: what C.G. Jung would have termed an "archetype." An archetype is that system of psychological organization—myths, rituals, shared dreams —wherein generations participate down through time as a way of maintaining the psychic health of the community. One of our most ancient archetypes common to all cultures is that of "The Way": how one enters the temple, addresses the group or elders, orders of succession, table manners, and so on. But more than simply ritualized behavior, "The Way" also illustrates that heroic—and necessarily psychological—journey each of us must make from birth, through adolescence and maturity, to old age and death. In the Occident, this psychic journey may be figuratively represented as the labyrinth from which Theseus confronts the Minotaur and, with the help of Ariadne, makes his escape; or Odysseus 20-year journey home; or Dante exploring the depths of Hell with Virgil as his guide. In the Orient, the archetype of "The Way" is summed up simply in the word "Tao." Nearly all disciplines in the East have centered their teaching around the concept of the Tao. In Japanese, when used as a word compound, "tao" becomes "*do*" as in *sado* (the way of tea), or *shodo* (the way of calligraphy). The word "dojo" (place of the way) is used as a suffix to refer to any of a number of training halls, such as *karate-dojo* (karate training hall).

The *roji* is a kind of psychological *dojo*, in that it establishes the ground to reaquaint the practitioner with the first time one entered the garden, or "the Way." To continually return to one's original nature as one begins practice is an ancient Buddhist tradition. The Zen master Rinzai, one of the more fearless investigators into human consciousness, once demanded of a novice monk: "Show me your face before your parents were born!" An old Buddhist expression ("*Shoshin Wasuru Bekarazu*") urges: "Don't forget your original mind." We may say that what is brought to mind as one enters the garden corresponds to what Suzuki Shunryu Roshi—founder of the San Francisco Zen Center—termed "beginner's mind." Suzuki Roshi equated one's original or "beginner's" mind with purity: a mind in a comfortable rut, he said, or one which has grown trite through mindless repetition, contaminates not only the mind itself, but also the teaching. A walk through the *roji* enables the guest to re-establish contact with the "beginner's mind," to begin again, as it were, and thus prepare one's spirit for the tea ceremony. T.S. Eliot succinctly expressed this experience of spiritual quest when he wrote in The Four Quartets:

> We shall not cease from exploration
> And the end of all our exploring
> Will be to arrive where we started
> And know the place for the first time.

When one washes one's hands and mouth at the *tsukubai* upon entering the *roji* , more is cleansed than simply portals of sensation: in Buddhistic terms, the mind is wiped clean of the dust of illusion. Having purified ourselves, what attitude should be assumed to maximize our appreciation of the tea ceremony? Certainly, one of acceptance and tranquility. In _Zen and Japanese Culture_, D.T.Suzuki writes that we are unable to accept things as they are or as they come to us: resistance means friction, friction is the source of all trouble. From the other side of the world, the noted Freudian analyst, Erich Fromm, wrote that human history is characterized by its struggle with nature: be it wilderness, animals, the soil, sex or dreams. He concludes by saying that a state of rest— as the Talmud would interpret the meaning of the Sabbath—is imperative to the understanding of our interaction with the world: work would be the antithesis. He writes: "In a state of rest, man antici- pates the state of human freedom that will be fulfilled eventually. The relationship of man and nature and of man and man is one of harmony [my emphasis], of peace, of noninterference. Work is a symbol of con- flict and disharmony; rest is an expression of dignity, peace and freedom." There is no evidence that Fromm had any experience of _chanoyu_. Yet, we see that the Occident is confronted with the same secular struggles, and is equipped with the inherent wisdom and history to guide it to the tea room as the Orient. A practice of rest, or meditation—"right effort," or "right mindfulness," according to the Sakyamuni's Eight-Fold Path—is essential to our spiritual sur- vival.

Zen, as an active practice, puts us squarely and unconditionally in the present. Our spiritual condition at any given moment is evident in our actions, be they cooking, washing, or praying. For the tea practitioner as well, it is considered an element of _wabi_ that one should place one's self, as it were, on display in the tea room. As with many arts associated with Zen, such as _shodo_ (calligraphy) or the _shakuhachi_ (bam- boo flute), the execution and manifestations of that art rely upon whatever spirituality is on hand at the moment: both in the mind of the artist as well as the beholder. The beauty of the garden, the tea room, and the preparation of tea is not to be understood strictly as physical acts: they are manifestations of the host's spirit.

Eihei Dogen (1200-1253), the renown teacher respon- sible for propagating Soto Zen in Japan informs us that the great Chinese teacher Zhaozhou once an- swered a novice monk's spiritual inquiries by simply replying: "Have some tea." Implied in this instruction is that nobility of endeavor and simplicity of resolve are often interrelated: that for all our grappling with problems spiritual or esoteric, it all can be concen- trated—to echo Sen-no-Rikyu—to a simple gesture of sipping some tea.

IV Kyoto's Gardens

The most important tea gardens in Kyoto are those directly connected with the tea schools: *Omote Senke* (the front house), *Mushanokoji Senke* (the middle house), and *Ura Senke* (the rear house). It was Rikyu's grandson, Sotan, who divided his estate among his three sons—with considerably more success than King Lear: all three schools continue to prosper today.

The *Senke* gardens, which introduce this book are from the Momoyama period (1568-1603). These gardens serve as classic examples of the garden aesthetics mentioned above. (Unfortunately, because of the important role the gardens play in the *Senke* tea schools, they are not regularly open for public inspection.)

The Imperial Villas offer other examples of exquisitely constructed tea gardens. *Katsura Rikyu* is one of most elaborate gardens in Japan, and is considered a pinnacle of Japanese landscape art. Construction began in the late 16th century, during the Edo period (1603-1868), possibly under the guidance of the landscape architect Kobori Enshu (1579-1647). According to one account, the military and political leader mentioned earlier, Hideyoshi Toyotomi, had something to do with its construction. In his later years, Hideyoshi, in an effort to bond his name with the royal family's, adopted Prince Toshihito as his own son. The *Katsura Rikyu* — sometimes called the "detached palace," or "Imperial Villa"—was originally to be Prince Toshihito's living quarters. Hideyoshi apparently chose the site along the Katsura River, from which the villa takes it's name. Another part of the legend suggests that in order to secure Kobori

Enshu as its architect, Hideyoshi had to submit to three conditions put forth by Enshu: that Enshu have complete control over the garden's construction; that there be no restraints on expense; and that no one be allowed to view the garden until it was finished. Hideyoshi agreed. The last condition proved tragic for Hideyoshi: he died before the garden's completion.

The gardens in the *Katsura Rikyu* are laid out according to the guidelines of the stroll garden: each turn of the path offers another perspective on the garden. As the tea ceremony was gaining popularity at the time, there are many tea houses on the grounds, and the architecture, design, and flora tend to be subdued. The tea house we see in the photographs [plates #13-16] is called the *Shokintei* tea house. The idyllic setting, as well as superb design, make it one of Japan's most famous buildings.

The *Sento Gosho,* also from the Edo period, was originally Emperor Gomizuno's (1596-1680) residence after his retirement. Unlike the *Katsura Rikyu*, it can be more confidently assumed that the architect Enshu was instrumental in the construction of the *Sento Gosho*. Although the *Sento Gosho*, like *Katsura Rikyu*, is designed as a stroll garden, (the tea garden it is part of a larger garden environment) the intimacy of the *roji* is maintained. Following the guidelines set down by Rikyu and Oribe, the *roji* still creates a feeling of intimacy among its guests. The tea house shown here [plates #17-18] is called the *Yushintei*.

With the exception of *Fushimi Inari Jinja* (see below) most of the gardens are connected with Buddhist temples (*ji*), and sub-temples (*in* or *an*). Among these, the sub-temples of *Daitoku-ji* are best represented here: *Koto-in* (1601), *Koho-an* (1621), and *Shinju-an* (1491). *Daitoku-ji's* connection with tea has been established from its beginning, since it was amply subsidized by Sakai merchants. For example, *Shinju-an* was founded as a memorial temple to Ikkyu by Owa Shirozaemon Sorin, an influential Sakai businessman. It's gardens to the east of the *hojo* (the head monk's quarters) were designed by the tea master Murata Shuko. *Koho-an* was originally the residence of Kobori Enshu, the most renown architect of his day. It contains a tea room, which is called *Bosen*. (*Bosen* literally translates as a solitary boat on the water. Something like "the old man and the sea," or more specifically, check out the painting "Solitary Fisherman on the River" by Ma Yuan circa 1220, Southern Sung dynasty.) *Koto-in* was established by Hosokawa Tadaoki (1563-1645), a famous *samurai* at the time. The tea house is named *Shokoken*. Also of note is the garden just south of the *hojo*. Two early abbots of *Koto-in* were the famous Zen masters Shiseido (teacher to Ungo Kiyo, 1582-1659), and Seigan Soi (1588-1661). While the tranquil setting makes *Koto-in* an enjoyable experience any time of the year, the maple trees in autumn are particularly beautiful.

Two Rinzai Zen temples outside of the *Daitoku-ji* compound are *Ryoan-ji* (1450), and *Saiho-ji*. (Both temples were destroyed—as was most of Kyoto—during the Onin wars, around 1469, and have undergone subsequent reconstruction.) *Saiho-ji* — sometimes called *Koke-dera*, the moss temple—is a Rinzai Zen temple located in southwest Kyoto. Although founded

in the eighth century, it's reconstruction was carried out by Muso Kokushi in 1339. The garden is representative of what the Jodo (Pure Land) sect of Buddhism would call a "Paradise Garden" in that the surroundings suggest the environs occupied by the Buddha Amidha. As such, *Saiho-ji* is often associated with the Pure Land sect of Buddhism. While justly famous for its moss garden, the construction of the *sukiya* (tea house) is worthy of appreciation as well. *Ryoan-ji,* one of Kyoto's most well known Zen temples, is home to the enigmatic rock garden (*kare sansui*) of—allegedly —Soami (1472-1525). What is often neglected amid the crush of camera-laden tourists is the striking stone basin, *chozubachi*, [plate #36], of the *Zorokuan* tea house behind the garden itself.

Another Rinzai temple featured here is *Toji-in*. Although founded in 1341 by Ashikaga Takauji, the present buildings were reconstructed in 1818. Along with other gardens mentioned here, the garden at *Toji-in* is said to have been designed by Muso Kokushi, but this is unsubstantiated. The tea house at the top of the hill is called *Seirentei*. Stephen Addiss, in his book *The Art of Zen*, relates an infamous tale connected with the temple *Toji-in*. It seems a monk, smitten by a young Kitano prostitute, had stolen a considerable sum of money in order to run away with his lover. Unfortunately, in making his escape, he left the money behind. In desperation, the lovers killed themselves, and temple became haunted by their ghosts. When Zen master Torei came to deliver a lecture at the temple, he was asked to exorcise the agitated spirits. Torei obliged. However, it seemed that only the monk's spirit was exorcised, because

V Conclusion

later the woman's spirit approached a monk in Mikawa saying she was a ghost, and unable to confront Torei directly because of his outstanding virtue. Torei held a special service which left her spirit fully at peace.

Other temples represented here include: *Ninna-ji*, a Shingon (esoteric) Buddhist temple, first established in 888 by the Emperor Kokaku, but completed by Emperor Uda a couple years later. *Honen-in* was named after Honen (1133-1212) who founded the Jodo (Pure Land) sect of Buddhism. The land which now contains *Koetsu-ji* was given to Honami Koetsu (1558-1637) by the shogun Tokugawa Ieyasu in 1615. Koestu himself was a tea master, calligrapher, potter, and accomplished sword maker. *Koestu-ji* is well known for the bamboo fence, *koetsugaki*, featured here. [plate #29] *Murin-an* was founded in 1896 by Prince Yamagata Aritomo, although Ogawa Jihei completed actual construction.

Fushimi Inari Jinja is a large shrine located in southern Kyoto, in the district from which it gets its name: Fushimi. It is probably best remembered for the countless *torii* which line its walkways. The *torii* —bright orange gateways—are offered by merchants and businesses as an added prayer for prosperity, as well as an insurance against bankruptcy. The symbol of the shrine is the fox, which may represent the cunning needed for any successful business venture. Be that as it may, every New Year's *Fushimi Inari Jinja* is jammed with patrons paying their annual respects.

So, how can we consider the future of tea? What relation can the tea garden and tea ceremony have with the burning demands of the twentieth century? The way to proceed is perhaps alluded to by Shoshitsu Sen XV, current head of The Urasenke Foundation of Kyoto and fifteenth generation Grand Tea Master after Rikyu. Writing in a recent afterword to Okakura's *The Book of Tea*, Shoshitsu Sen XV concludes that tea must take a broader perspective, in the face of "near-inconceivable destructive power, and the steady erosion of the environment, poisoning the air we breathe and the water we drink." One of the basic assumptions of tea is one's awareness of location: how one is placed in relation to the garden, the tea room, and fellow guests. It has become increasingly difficult to ignore our relation to events outside the walls of the tea garden: events which threaten our very sense of location.

All spiritual endeavors and experience share one thing—perhaps the only thing—in common: they are extremely portable. For the practitioner, the portable tea service, "*chabako*," allows a tea ceremony to be performed practically anywhere. Hence, everywhere becomes the *roji*: the path that brings us to a consciousness which embodies the four qualities of harmony, reverence, purity, and tranquility. An aesthetic or religious practice which does not extend outside the *dojo*, or training ground, brings into question the validity of such practice. Muso Kokushi maintained that parts of the empirical truth perceived in a garden however small, manifests a higher truth of Buddhism, that transcends the reality of the garden. The mind cleansed by the *roji*, and inspired by the tea, must certainly not be limited to the confines of the cere-mony. As one's experience of tea deepens, one is challenged with the kind of consciousness which is appropriate to the tea room, as well as our daily lives. This enrichment of aesthetic appreciation, in turn, begins to slowly inform our daily behavior so that ordinary acts, such as washing dishes or changing diapers, become infused with a profundity otherwise alien to the untrained heart and mind.

From the world of tea we learn the portability of consciousness: of what KIND of mind can be brought into play in the myriad situations which confront us in daily life. The tea garden becomes the larger field for the rejuvenation of spiritual values, which today have become synonymous with the natural world of earth, plants, water and air. A walk through the *roji* becomes a climb to a 10,000 ft. summit!

It was Dogen who stressed two levels of commu-nion of man and nature: the perception of geological nature, and the religious experience of geological nature as a tangible manifestation of higher [Budd-hist] truth. In the tea garden, man's exclusion of Nature disqualifies the garden from assuming the dimensions of another Eden: the *roji* seeks not to mimic paradise. Although paradise is often the first impression one has of the tea garden, Zen instructs us that paradise too is illusion. Whereas Zen does not avoid a confrontation with psychological wilderness, the tea garden presumes a tranquility and harmony not usually associated with Nature (except in an anachronistically Pastoral sense). On the contrary, as mentioned, wilderness—psychological and physical—in the garden is conspicuous in its absence. By bring-ing a respect for wild systems (bio-spheres) to play upon the mind, the tea garden can be infused with a wildness through the care and gratitude of its visi-tors. In this way, the ideals of *wabi* and the imperfect environment which we have created, contribute to a more complete understanding of our place, and our actions, in the garden.

The courage required to maintain harmony, rever-ence, purity, and tranquility in the tea garden can be, must be expanded to include the larger garden of our planet. A cultivated appreciation of the tea garden brings with it a cultivation, as Shoshitsu Sen XV writes, "of human culture transcending the bound-aries of nations." The implication is obvious: one must not limit what the mind can bring to the tea garden, nor constrict the possible interpretations of the garden outside its walls. By reintroducing wilder-ness into our daily mind we can rejuvenate the tea garden: truly a worthy gift to the future. We bring to the tea garden a mind which is inspired and informed by wilderness, as well as a respect for our planet's bio-systems. What we can take with us from the garden is a sense of rest, an at-ease-ness, or at-one-ment (atonement!) with Nature which is harmonious, tranquil, and allows our environment to prosper unhindered by excessively greedy notions of progress. Entering the inner world of the *roji*, humbly crouch-ing before the *tsukubai*, cleansing our hands and mouth—these actions have now become synonymous with entering and acting in the outer world. The two are not different: that which we discover at the sum-mit we realize greeted us at the trailhead.

Notes on the Photographs

1. Omote Senke (Muromachi period)

As the entrance to the *roji*, this "crawling through space" or *rojiguchi*, is used by the guests to contribute to their sense of humility. Note the gradual increase in height of the stones leading to the passage-way.

2. Omote Senke

The perspective of this photograph is the opposite of plate #1: we are now looking back toward the *roji guchi*. While the *roji* is usually subdued in color, note how fallen pine needles have been gathered at the base of the tree to the left. As spring approaches, the circle will become smaller and smaller until it disappears.

3. Omote Senke

We now approach the entrance to the inner *roji*. In the foreground we see the stepping stones, *tobi ishi*, leading us to the "crawling-in passage," *nijiriguchi*.

4. Omote Senke

This *sukiya*, or tea house, is named *Tensetsu-do*. The stepping stones gracefully protrude from the velvety moss. The *nijiriguchi* is visible to the right.

5. Ura Senke (Muromachi period)

This long shot is of the flagstones, or cobblestones, *shiki ishi*, leading from the waiting area to the middle gate. The narrowness of the pathway enhances the feeling of introspection in the guest.

6. Ura Senke

The inner *roji*: note the *tsukubai* to the right with

the ladle (*tsukubai-bishaku*). A moss laden lantern, *toro*, is visible behind the *tsukubai* area.

7. Ura Senke

We approach the tea room. Notice the larger stepping stone which leads one to the *nijiriguchi*, as well as the broom hanging to the left. Aside from the sunshine, the only bright color in the garden are the fallen leaves gathered to the left foreground.

8. Ura Senke

In an otherwise subdued environment, again the fallen red and yellow leaves provide a streak of color, which in themselves imply the impermanence of life, and the cycle of seasons. The leaves are accentuated by the dark grey of the stones and the brown of the "spicebush hedge," *kuromoji gaki*.

9. Mushanokoji Senke (Muromachi period)

Here we see a subtle arrangement of flagstones, *shiki ishi*, which winds its way through the **Mushanokoji Senke** garden. While abundant moisture is implied by the lushness of the foliage, water (except that in the *chozubachi*) is absent.

10. Mushanokoji Senke

This photograph shows the middle gate (*naka kuguri*) separating the inner and outer *roji*. Not considered to be a true gate in any functional manner, the middle gate serves as a reminder of the spiritual steps one takes to the tea room. It is here that the host welcomes the guest, *mukae tsuke*.

11. Mushanokoji Senke

Here we have the essentials of the tea garden in a concentrated form: in the background is the *tsukubai* and the *ishidoro* lantern; after ritual washing it is just a few steps to the entrance of the tea room. We can visualize the steps of the guest: in such a small space such steps resemble an archaic dance of purification.

12. Yabunouchi Shoke (Muromachi period)

This photograph shows the delicate arrangement of the *tsukubai*; a large flat stone, *maeishi*, to crouch upon; the *chozubachi* surrounded by ferns; and a lantern, *toro*, to the upper left. The lanterns are of the *ikekomi* style, in that they are without a pedestal and rest very low to the ground.

13. Katsura Rikyu (Edo period)

A waiting area (*machiai*). Notice the large stone (*kyaku ishi*) before the bench, *koshikake*, for the guests to rest their feet upon. After leaving the waiting area, the guest proceeds down the long *shiki ishi*, or flagstones, to the inner *roji*.

14. Katsura Rikyu

From this perspective, one can appreciate the intricate dimensions of the **Katsura Rikyu** stroll garden: the pine tree perfectly reflected in the pond; two flat stone bridges connecting different areas of the garden; and the *Shokintei* tea house in the distance. The pebbled shore of the pond (*ariso*) is meant to represent a natural coastline.

15. Katsura Rikyu

Here we see the long stone bridge which brings us to the *Shokintei* tea house. The *tsukubai* is located on the far shore to the right of the bridge. It is difficult to see because it is of the *nagare chozu* style, which means that, instead of drawing water from a stone basin, water is taken directly from the pond.

16. Katsura Rikyu

Another *machiai* of the **Katsura Rikyu** garden. Of particular note is the arrangement of stepping stones (*tobi ishi*) amid the gravel in the foreground. Usually, the stones are placed in moss, so here we have a quite dynamic arrangement which highlights the placement of the stones while maintaining a subdued atmosphere.

17. Sento Gosho (Edo period: 1630)

A beautifully proportioned "middle gate" (*naka kuguri*) which is highlighted by the rustic quality of the bamboo fence and the arrangement of the *tobi ishi*. The thatched roof style of *naka kuguri* is called *kayabuki*. From the threshold of the gate we can see the *nijiriguchi* entrance to the tea room.

18. Sento Gosho

After passing through the *naka kuguri*, the guest proceeds to the *Yushintei* tea house. To the right, is a stone lantern, *ishi doro*, overlooking the *tsukubai*.

19. Sento Gosho

Shown here is the *tsukubai* and *toro* which are located in front of the *Seikatei* tea house of the **Sento Gosho**.

20. Sento Gosho

This majestic stone lantern, *ishidoro*, is located behind the *Seikatei* tea house. It is slightly removed from the main part of the garden, but adds a subtle touch to the *roji* for those who seek it out.

21. Koto-in (Momoyama period: 1601)

The paper screens, *shoji*, of the *Shokoken* tea house, have been parted to reveal an exquisite scene of the stepping stones—which seem to lose themselves in the garden. In the background is a stone lantern nestled among bush bamboo, *sasa*. It is a time when the brilliant colors of autumn impose themselves upon the otherwise softer tones of the garden.

22. Koto-in

The interior of the *Shokoken* tea house at *Koto-in*. The host enters from the small passage (*nijiriguchi*) in the far corner of the room. The brazier, *ro*, and the kettle, *kama*, for boiling the water, are in the center of the tea room, *chashitsu*. The subdued quality of the walls, combined with the soft light from the *shoji*, create an tranquil atmosphere for the guest and host.

23. Koho-an (Edo period: 1621)

From this perspective, the elevated *chozubachi* is accented by the dark wood of the tea house on one side, and the black stones on the other. Rather than "crouching" to wash our hands and mouth, this wash basin suggests more of a bowing motion: the feeling of humility is sustained.

24. Koho-an

This *tsukubai*, and stone lantern (*ishidoro*) have a wider, more open setting than one is accustomed to. The washing area is of the "well" style, *ido tsukubai*.

25. Shinju-an (Muromachi period: 1491)

This tea house was added to the temple in 1638. The path to the tea house reminds one of a stroll through an evergreen forest. It was built as a memorial to the tea master Ikkyu.

26. Shinju-an

The interior of the tea house. The *ro* is visible in the center of the room. Like the tea room of *Koto-in*, this one is of a subdued nature.

27. Korin-in (Muromachi period)

An unusual instance of water used in the *roji*, this garden is nonetheless gracefully laid out. Again, the close proximity of the *tsukubai* to the *nijiriguchi* is apparent.

28. Saio-in (Muromachi period: 1584)

From this perspective we can trace the movements of the guests as they enter the tea room. The roof provides an enclosure and shading which enhance the intimacy of the tea house.

29. Koetsu-ji (Edo period)

The bamboo fence (*koetsugaki*) seen against a backdrop of brilliant autumn leaves. This fence is said to have been constructed by Honami Koestu himself.

30. Jikko-in (Edo period)

The pattern of the *tobi ishi* before the waiting area is dramatically highlighted in the snow. While not necessarily subdued in tone, the snow creates a tranquility of its own—conducive to a cup of tea.

31. Hokyo-ji (Kamakura period)

From this perspective, our path to the tea room is clear; our steps are sure. It is easy to visualize going to the *tsukubai* to wash, then turning to enter the tea house.

32. Honen-in (Edo period: 1680)

While perhaps not an actual *roji* in the traditional sense, here we see how the *tsukubai* is delicately nestled near the pond. One has a glimpse of the pond prior to entering the tea room, which in turn makes one's spirit more receptive to the subtleties of the tea.

33. Keishun-in (Edo period: 1632)

The middle gate, and the stepping stones are discreetly placed among the abundant foliage. Once one has entered the *roji*, one has the impression of entering a fathomless world.

34. Toji-in (Muromachi period)

Snow adds another dimension to the qualities of the tea garden. A stillness and silence, which elude other seasons, are in abundance in winter. The turbulence which characterized the age in which the garden was constructed (the Onin wars) is reflected in the agitated lay out of the garden.

35. Ninna-ji (Heian period: 888)

Coming before this *tsukubai* is much like one would imagine the Oracle at Delphi: the design of the stone is not rustic, but has more of a pattern reminiscent of Western culture.

36. Ryoan-ji (Muromachi period: 1450)

The stylized *chozubachi* of the *Zorokuan* tea house behind the famous rock garden at *Ryoan-ji*. The Chinese characters can be read as "Realizing what is enough"("*ware tada taru o shiru*").

37. Saiho-ji (Kamakura period)

While often upstaged by its moss garden, the *Saiho-ji* tea house must not be over-looked. The view of the garden is best appreciated in late spring when the rains bring out the lushness of the moss.

38. Saiho-ji

The tea garden seeks to provide a clear path for the guest to walk. The *tsukubai* entreats us to purify ourselves before continuing on to the tea room. In this photograph, we are looking back from where we came in plate #37.

39. Murin-an (Meiji period: 1895)

Here, the autumn leaves are like an umbrella of light or fire, hanging precariously over the garden. How many times has a walk into the present moment been a walk through flames?

40. Saiko-ji

The *tobi ishi* here invite one to glide across them to

the washing area. The subtle spacing of the stones is powerful in its understatement. Our attention is not drawn to the stones—or our footsteps—but to our movement through the garden, almost like a spirit moving through space.

41. Ryosoku-in (Edo period)

The two lanterns, separated by the plants and the pond, suggest another communication of aesthetics, which go beyond the confines of the garden. The lantern in the foreground is of the *ikekomi* style, without a pedestal, while the one in the background is a standing *ishidoro* style.

42. Kodai-ji (Edo period: 1605)

Here again we follow the stones to the tea room, past the *ishidoro* lantern. Notice the Buddha figures carved at the base of the lantern: this tradition of ornamenting lanterns with images of the Buddha was developed by Oribe, Rikyu's disciple.

43. Kodai-ji

The subtlety of this *tsukubai* is enhanced by the expectation of our entrance into the *Karakasa-tei* tea room. The stone placed before the *chozubachi* is wide enough to allow two people to wash simultaneously. In actuality, the extra space is for a servant who would hold an umbrella or otherwise assist a noble in their ablutions.

44. Kodai-ji

This is the spectacular ceiling to the *Karakasa-tei* tea house of **Kodai-ji**. Spread out like an umbrella, or

the spokes of a wheel, the allusion to the ever-turning wheel of the dharma is unmistakable.

45. Kainyo-an (Momoyama period)

From here, we have a view of the middle gate, the stone lantern, the washing area, and the stepping stones. While sipping our tea, we can retrace our steps which brought us to this moment.

46. Fushimi-inari Shrine (Nara period: 711)

The tea garden is not usually associated with Shinto shrines, and yet the garden here is hardly considered to be out of place. What is striking is the layout of the stones, and the stone lantern, in an abundance of soft green.

47. Higashi Hongan-ji (Edo period)

A slightly elevated *chozubachi*, with ladle (*tsukubai-bishaku*). Like the basin at **Koho-an**, the feeling of humility is reinforced with a bowing motion, as opposed to the usual crouching.

Front Cover: *Mushanokoji Senke Roji (Muromachi period)*

This middle gate, *nakakuguri*, is of the *hiwadabuki* style: thatched with cypress, *hinoki*, bark.

Back Cover: *Omote Senke (Muromachi period)*

The interior of the *Fushi-an* tea room. Slightly brighter than other tea rooms, this one nevertheless maintains a feeling of quiet and simplicity.

Glossary

● *ai-no-gaki*

This is the barrier located on either side of the "middle gate." It can be either a hedge, or somekind of shrubbery, or a fence, usually made of bamboo. [compare plates #17 and #10]

● *chabako*

Literally "tea box." This is a portable tea service includies all essential tools for performing a ceremony anywhere.

● *chisenkaiyu*

The stroll garden. In this landascape gardening technique, the view and perspective of the garden changes as one walks around the garden, usually by following a predetermined path.

● *chozubachi*

This is the stone basin used for holding pure water with which guests cleanse hands and mouth.

● *hanayome shugyo*

This is a kind of bridal training. Young women practice various forms of cultural arts — tea and *ikebana* among them—as a sign of good breeding. Often practiced in order to secure a husband as much as for the art form itself.

● *ikebana*

Literally, "living flowers," this refers to the art of flower arrangement: a highly refined art which stresses color, balance, and symbolic reference of the flowers.

● *ikekomi*

This is a style of lantern which has no pedestal: it has an appearance of simply sitting on the ground. [see plate #41]

● *ishi doro*

Stone lantern.

● *kakemono*

This is the hanging scroll in the aclove, *tokonoma*, in the tea room: sometimes a ink landscape of a few brush strokes, or a calligraphy of zen origin.

● *kama*

A kettle used for boiling water for tea, specifically iron.

● *kansu*

Another name for a kettle.

● *kare nagare*

Literally, "dry stream," this landscaping technique suggests moving water by the careful use of sand, gravel, or stones. The illusion of waves can be implied by how the sand is raked.

● *kare sansui*

The dry rock garden favored by many Zen temples. Most notably are the gardens of *Ryoan-ji*, *Nanzen-ji*, and *Daitoku-ji*.

● *katana kake*

Located near the enterance to the tea room, these are hooks where guests can hang their swords. Today, mostly for decorative use—but not always.

● *kaya buki*

This style of "middle gate" has a thatched roof. [see plate #17]

● *kyaku ishi*

The stones upon which one rest one's feet while waiting to be shown to the *chashitsu*. These stones are arranged so that the main guests get to rest their feet on the largest stone.

● *koshikake machiai*

The bench for waiting guests to sit on, part of the "outer roji." Special stones (*kyaku ishi*) are placed in front of the *koshikake* to distinguish the main guest from regular guests.

● *machiai*
This is the waiting room, or waiting area. The *machiai* contains the bench, *koshikake*, and the lavatory, *setchin*.

● *mae ishi*
This is the broad stone placed just before the *chozubachi*. Guests "crouch" on this stone to wash their hands and mouth before proceeding to the tea room. [see plate #12]

● *mukae tsuke*
This describes the host's greeting of the guests at the "middle gate," *naka kuguri*. In a formal tea ceremony, the host meets the guest half-way between the outer and inner *roji*, and serves as an escort to the tea room.

● *naka dachi*
Relaxation of legs. [see *seiza*]

● *naka kuguri*
The middle gate separating the inner and outer *roji*. It is here that the host greets the guests (*mukae tsuke*) in a formal tea ceremony.

● *nijiriguchi*
Literally, the "crawling-in entrance." This is the small passage into the tea room, though usually only for decorative use these days. In the photographs of the tea houses, look for a little brown door just off to the right [see plates #4, #7, and #18]; off to the left [see plate #28]; or in the center [see plate #31]. *Aprés vous*.

● *niju roji*
This descirbes a garden with an outer and inner *roji* only. [see *taju roji*]

● *nobedan*

This is another word for flagstones, or cobblestones. [see *shiki ishi*]

● *ro*
The sunken brazier in the middle of the tea room, used for boiling water for tea. [see plate #22]

● *roji*
Literally "dewy ground." This is the smaller contained garden within the larger grounds of the tea garden, or more generally, *roji* refers to the tea garden itself.

● *sao ishi*
A lantern's "stem" stone which is inserted directly into the ground. On top of the *sao ishi* is placed a stone or iron lantern.

● *seiza*
A posture consisting of sitting on one's knees and ankles, with spine erect. Called *Vajrasan* (Diamond pose) in hatha yoga, it is usually perceived as a form of punishment for beginners.

● *Senke*
This ubiquitous word in the tea world stands for the family or house of *Sen*. Beginning with *Sen-no-Rikyu*, the family line has continued for 18 generations to the present day. The current *UraSenke* Grand Tea Master is Sen Soshitsu XV.

● *seppuku*
A ritualized form of suicide. (*Harakiri*—"belly slitting"—is its vuglar expression.) Originally an honorable means, among the *samurai* class, of absolving one's disgrace, Yukio Mishima demonstrated in 1970 that *seppuku* may yet have a place in the twentieth century.

● *setchin*
Lavatory. This modest building, located within the

waiting area, is usually for decorative purposes only, depending on the condition of the guests when they arrive to or depart from the tea room. If used in ernest, sand is sometimes employed to breakdown waste.

● **shiki ishi**

Flagstones. These are clustered into square groups, like cobblestones, which connect the more loosely arranged stepping stones, *tobi ishi*. [see plate #5 and #9]

● **shoji**

Sliding doors which are of a simple lattice work, and covered with paper. More for an announcement of privacy rather than to actually block out noise or cold.

● **soto roji**

The outer garden, usually wider and airier than the inner (*uchi roji*) garden.

● **taju roji**

This would describe a garden which has multiple *roji*. The **Omote Senke** garden for example, has an inner, outer, and middle *roji*.

● **tatami**

3'x6' rice straw matting used as a floor in many Japanese rooms. A tatami mat is counted as "*jo*." For example, a three mat room,"*san-jo*," of a four-and-a-half mat room, "*yo-jo-han*," etc.

● **teishu**

The host of a tea ceremony.

● **tobi ishi**

The stepping stones which lead one through the roji . They are often arranged in groups of five or seven, and are spaced in such a way as to influence the pace of one's physical steps to the tea room.

● **tokonoma**

The small alcove in the tea room which usually contains a hanging scroll or picture, *kakemono*, and small art object to be admired after having had tea.

● **tome ishi**

Stones which have been tied with thin black rope which serve as signs that one may not proceed any further.

● **toro**

Lanterns placed throughout the garden, most often near the *tsukubai*, and along the stone steps.

● **tsukubai**

The washing area in the garden. It contains the stone water basin (*chozubachi*), as well as the stones, (*mae ishi*), lantern, (*toro*), and plants which surround the basin. There are several kinds of *tsukubai*: *ori tsukubai*, "inclining"; *nagare tsukubai*, "stream" [see plate #15]; or *ido tsukubai*, "well" [see plate #47].

● **tsukubai-bishaku**

The wooden, or bamboo, ladle which lies across the stone water basin, *chozubachi*, which is to be used for rinsing one's hands and mouth. No *chozubachi* is complete without one.

● **tsukubau**

Literally "to crouch," hence the name given to the area for cleansing hands and mouth, *tsukubai*: one should combine a humble attitude along with the act of purifying oneself before entering the tea room.

● **uchi roji**

The inner garden, darker and more confined than the outer (*soto*) garden.

Further Reading

- *Zen and Japanese Culture* D.T.Suzuki. New Jersey: Princeton University Press, 1959.
- *The Book of Tea* Kakuzo Okakura. Tokyo: Kodansha, 1989.
- *Zen Mind, Beginners Mind* Shunryu Suzuki. Tokyo: Weatherhill, 1970.
- *Turtle Island* Gary Snyder. New York: New Directions, 1974.
- *Ikkyu and The Crazy Cloud Anthology* Sonja Arntzen. Tokyo: University of Tokyo Press, 1986.
- *Moon in a Dewdrop*: *Writings of Zen Master Dogen*. ed. Kazuaki Tanahashi. San Francisco: North Point Press, 1985.
- *Secret Teachings in the Art of Japanese Gardens* David A. Slawson. Tokyo: Kodansha International, 1987.
- *The Art of Zen* Stephen Addiss. New York: Abrams, 1989.
- *Tea Ceremony* Kaisen Iguchi, trans. by John Clark. Osaka:Hoikusha, 1975.
- *Cha-no yu: The Japanese Tea Ceremony* A.L. Sadler. Tokyo: Tuttle, 1962. (first edition 1933)
- *Historical Chanoyu* Plutschow, Herbert E. Tokyo: The Japan Times, 1986.
- *Zen Gardens: Kyoto's Nature Enclosed* Tom Wright and Katsuhiko Mizuno. Kyoto: Suiko Books, 1990.
- *A Guide to the Gardens of Kyoto* Marc Treib and Ron Herman. Tokyo: Shufunotomo Co., Ltd.,1980.

The Author

Preston L. Houser was born in Salina, Kansas, and reared in the San Francisco Bay Area. He lives with his wife and young son in Kyoto.

Mr. Houser first came to Japan in 1981 to pursue his interests in Zen Buddhism and the bamboo flute, *shakuhachi*. As a musician, he concentrates on the traditional repertoire of solo pieces associated with the—now defunct—Zen sect of the *Fuke-shu*, as well as ensemble work with *koto* and *shamisen*. He has performed in concerts and festivals in Japan and America.

Mr. Houser holds a Master's degree in English Literature from San Francisco State University, with an emphasis on Shakespeare studies and Jungian psychology. Currently, he is a part-time university lecturer.

The Photographer

Mizuno Katsuhiko was born in Kyoto in 1941. Since 1969 he has been working to capture the beauty of Kyoto's natural scenery, and cultural heritage. Among his over thirteen publications are: Kyoto Tsubo Niwa (Miniature Gardens), published by Mitsumura Suiko Shoin, in 1980; Shiki Kyoto (The Four Seasons of Kyoto), published by Mitsumura Suiko Shoin, in 1983; Zen Gardens, published by Mitsumura Suiko Shoin, in 1990; Masterspieces of Garden Art in Kyoto, published by Kyoto Shoin, in 1991.

Mr. Mizuno has written numerous editorials on traditional Japanese culture. He is also a member of the Japan Photographers Association.